MYSTERIES OF
EASTER ISLAND

Laura Hamilton Waxman

Lerner Publications ◆ Minneapolis

Lerner Publications Company
A division of Lerner Publishing Group, Inc.
241 First Avenue North
Minneapolis, MN 55401 USA

For reading levels and more information, look up this title at www.lernerbooks.com.

Main body text set in Aptifer Slab LT Pro Regular 11.5/18.
Typeface provided by Linotype AG.

Library of Congress Cataloging-in-Publication Data

Names: Waxman, Laura Hamilton, author.
Title: Mysteries of Easter Island / Laura Hamilton Waxman.
Description: Minneapolis : Lerner Publications, 2017. | Series: Ancient
    mysteries | Includes bibliographical references and index.
Identifiers: LCCN 2016049274 (print) | LCCN 2016050738 (ebook) |
    ISBN 9781512440157 (lb : alk. paper) | ISBN 9781512449174 (eb pdf)
Subjects: LCSH: Easter Island—History—Juvenile literature. | Easter
    Island—Antiquities—Juvenile literature.
Classification: LCC F3169 .W39 2017 (print) | LCC F3169 (ebook) | DDC
    996.18—dc23

LC record available at https://lccn.loc.gov/2016049274

Manufactured in the United States of America
1-42277-26134-3/24/2017

TABLE OF CONTENTS

ENCOUNTERING A MYSTERY

On Easter in 1722, a fleet of three Dutch ships was exploring the southeastern Pacific Ocean. The fleet's commander, Jacob Roggeveen, was searching for an undiscovered continent that the Dutch thought might exist in the area. Instead, Roggeveen and his men spotted a small island. Roggeveen named it Easter Island.

As the Dutch ships drew closer to the island, the sailors noticed smoke rising into the air. The smoke signaled that people were living there. But the island itself looked empty, with dry grass and few trees. When Roggeveen and his men came ashore, they met a community of perhaps two thousand people. They also saw something that struck them with awe: hundreds of giant stone statues.

THE STATUES OF EASTER ISLAND

The statues had enormous heads with large noses, staring eyes, and wide mouths. Many of the statues stood side by side along the island's coast. Their backs were to the sea, and their faces looked in toward the middle of the island.

A group of statues stands side by side along the coast of Easter Island.

Roggeveen and one of his men look at a statue after landing on Easter Island in this twentieth-century illustration.

Roggeveen and his men had many questions. How had the islanders carved such enormous statues without metal tools? And how had they moved the giant stone carvings around the island? The islanders had few firm answers. Most stories about the statues had been lost or forgotten. The statues of Easter Island were one of the world's great unsolved mysteries.

CHAPTER 1
A MYSTERIOUS HISTORY

Over the years, researchers called **archaeologists** have worked to **excavate** Easter Island to try to uncover its past and solve its mysteries. They have dug below the newer, upper layers of soil and sand to get to the ancient layers below. There they have discovered some clues to Easter Island's past.

HUMAN SETTLEMENT

Easter Island is a remote place. The closest continent, South America, is 2,237 miles (3,600 kilometers) away. Its closest neighbor, Pitcairn Island, lies 1,100 miles (1,770 km) away. So how did humans end up in such an isolated place?

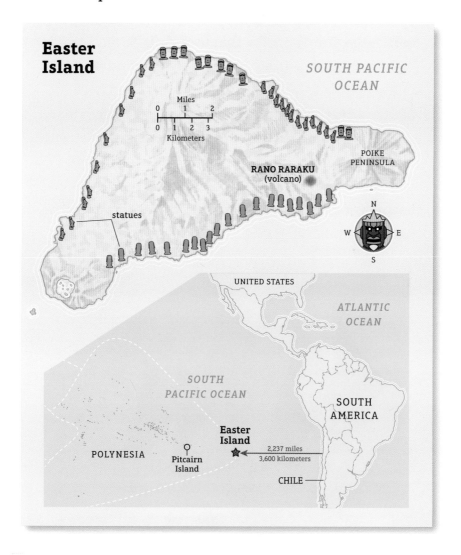

Archaeologists believe that the people who first settled the island came from Polynesia. This large cluster of islands is in the southern and central Pacific Ocean. It is not known exactly which island the people of Easter Island came from, but it may have been more than 3,000 miles (4,828 km) away. The ancient Polynesian people were skilled sea travelers. They built large, sturdy canoes that used sails.

At some point, a group of traveling Polynesians found their way to Easter Island. Researchers have used radiocarbon dating to try to find out when. This scientific method measures carbon, an element present in the remains of living things such as bones, teeth, and hair. The amount of carbon in these remains goes down over time. This helps scientists determine how old the remains might be.

In 2011 sailors set off on a journey from Hawaii to San Francisco using traditional Polynesian navigation methods and these canoes, modeled after traditional Polynesian designs.

DIG DEEP!

Scientists have used **DNA** testing on excavated human bones from Easter Island. This testing confirms that the early settlers were Polynesian. Scientists have also studied the bones of animals that the early islanders hunted and ate. These bones show that the island was once home to birds such as owls, parrots, and herons. None of these native animals still live on the island.

Through radiocarbon dating, scientists found evidence that humans may have arrived at Easter Island as early as 400 CE. But other evidence suggested that humans didn't arrive until 800 or even 1200.

FARMERS, HUNTERS, AND SCULPTORS

Whenever the island's newcomers did arrive, they entered a land covered in trees. The islanders were a farming people, so they cleared the trees from the island to grow crops. They also hunted the island's birds and sea animals for food. The new settlers thrived in their new home. Over time, their population may have reached as many as twenty thousand.

At some point, the islanders discovered a source of stone in the crater of an old volcano. They used this stone to carve the mysterious giant statues. This activity might have started as early as 700. The last statues were likely made in the seventeenth century. By then the islanders had made about nine hundred statues.

A partially carved statue lies abandoned in the volcano crater.

This bare, grassy part of the island was probably once covered in trees and was full of life.

A CHANGED LANDSCAPE

By the time Europeans arrived on the island, most of the island's trees had disappeared and fewer people lived there. Researchers are not sure why civilization on the island seems to have collapsed. One idea is that with fewer trees, there were fewer roots to hold down the soil. Over time, wind **eroded** the soil and it became less fertile. The island became a dry grassland. The islanders likely used up the island's resources for food, and without enough food, the island's population also shrunk. Disease, warfare, and destructive rats may have also played a role. But while the trees and people disappeared, the mysterious statues remained.

CHAPTER 2
MAKING MONUMENTS

Over the last hundred years, archaeologists have wondered why the Easter Island statues were made, why they are so big, and why there are so many of them. The answers to these questions may never be fully understood, but through study, archaeologists have come up with some ideas.

THE PURPOSE OF THE STATUES

Ancient Polynesians greatly respected their dead ancestors. They often built **monuments** to honor them, similar to modern gravestones. This was especially true of important chiefs or other leaders. Many of the monuments were made of wood, but some were made of stone. Many archaeologists believe that the Easter Island statues served a purpose similar to other Polynesian monuments. The large size of the statues may represent the importance of the ancestors they honored.

Statues stand along the coast on platforms known as *ahus*. *Ahu* is also the word for a shrine, or sacred ceremonial place.

Researchers have dug around this statue, revealing parts that had been underground.

MYTH ALERT!

For a long time, people thought that many of Easter Island's statues were giant heads without **torsos**. That was especially true of statues farther inland from the coast. But archaeologists who have dug around those statues have discovered the truth. All the statues appear to have torsos. Some just became buried under layers of dirt over time.

CARVING STONE

The islanders probably built the statues inside an old volcano known as Rano Raraku. Ash from the volcano hardened to create stone that chipped away easily, making it ideal for sculpting. A person would still need sharp tools to carve it, though. The ancient islanders did not have any metal tools. But archaeologists have uncovered ancient stone tools, which means that the islanders knew how to make and use sharp **chisels**. One study revealed that twenty people could carve a statue in one year with stone tools.

An archaeologist examines a *toki*, a stone handheld chisel used to carve the statues.

CHAPTER 3
MOVING MONUMENTS

The statues on Easter Island vary in size. On average, they weigh 14 tons (13 metric tons) and are 13 feet (4 meters) tall. The largest statues are even bigger, up to 72 feet (22 m) tall and 165 tons (150 metric tons).

The statues are scattered around the island. About one-third were moved up to 11 miles (18 km) from the volcano to the coasts. There they stand on stone platforms that the islanders also made. The rest of the statues appear to have been abandoned at the volcano or along ancient roads. Some archaeologists believe these statues may have been too difficult to move.

Many people living on Easter Island work as tour guides or help archaeologists with their research. Tour guide Tito Atan learned about the history and traditions of Easter Island from his grandmother.

MYTH ALERT!

A famous myth about Easter Island is that aliens from outer space once lived there. Swiss author Erich von Däniken suggested this idea in the 1960s. Däniken believed the aliens were space explorers who had gotten stranded on Easter Island. He wrote that they used their advanced technology to produce the statues. The statues were left behind when the aliens were rescued by their own kind. However, the work of archaeologists has presented much more likely theories about Easter Island. No one has ever found evidence of alien activity there.

TESTING IDEAS

Over the years, people have come up with different ideas about how the giant statues were moved. They tested those ideas by trying to move the statues with these methods. Some of these experiments failed. But others showed how the islanders might have moved the statues.

Thor Heyerdahl, an archaeologist from Norway, completed one of the most successful experiments during an expedition from 1955 to 1956. He attached a statue to a wooden sled. Then people pulled the sled with rope, which could have been made from native trees. This experiment showed that 180 people could move one of the smaller statues. But moving a big statue would take up to 1,500 people.

Heyerdahl *(right)* believed that the islanders used wooden sleds like this one to move the statues around the island.

WALKING STATUES

In 2011 American archaeologists Terry Hunt and
Carl Lipo decided to test another idea. They had been
thinking about a famous Easter Island legend that
says the statues had walked. The men wondered if this
meant that the statues were moved in a way that was
similar to walking.

Lipo and Hunt used a **replica** of one of the smaller
statues on Easter Island. It was 10 feet (3 m) tall
and weighed 5 tons (4.5 metric tons). The two men
organized small teams of people to move the statue.

Teams of people pull on
ropes to test Lipo and Hunt's
theory about how the statues
were moved.

Lipo and Hunt successfully moved a statue more than 100 yards (91 m) using this method.

The teams pulled on a simple system of ropes attached to the upright statue. Their pulling moved the statue forward in a rocking motion. This motion made it look as if the statue was walking. And this method worked with as few as eighteen people. Lipo and Hunt wrote about their findings in a book published in 2012. They believe their method makes more sense than Heyerdahl's. But no one has been able to prove exactly how the statues were moved.

CHAPTER 4
PRESERVING HISTORY

In the late nineteenth century, Easter Island became part of Chile. To protect the statues from damage, Chile has turned the island into a national park called Rapa Nui National Park. Rapa Nui is what native islanders called Easter Island. The island is home to about five thousand people. About half are native islanders. The other half are Chileans.

Recently, climate change on Earth has caused sea levels to rise. Higher seas mean higher waves lapping the shores of Easter Island. The waves are slowly eroding the ancient stone platforms that support the statues along the coasts. If the platforms erode too much, the statues will fall into the sea. Centuries of wind and rain have also damaged the statues throughout the island. Scientists have recently developed a chemical that preserves stone. Islanders and archaeologists are working to apply this chemical to the statues for protection.

A fallen statue lies near the shore.

Markings are visible on the torso of a statue Heyerdahl dug up in 1955. He thought that these markings were similar to markings found on objects from South America and that this meant the people of Easter Island were South American.

DIG DEEP!

The statues whose torsos are buried underground have been protected from wind and rain. An archaeologist named Jo Anne Van Tilburg is working with islanders to dig around those statues to try to learn more about their origins. Van Tilburg found markings on the statues that appear to be canoes. She believes the markings were a kind of signature. They may have shown who made the statue or whose ancestor the statue honored.

Van Tilburg *(right)* uses a grid to measure a statue for a computer image.

RECORDING HISTORY

Archaeologists and islanders are also making a detailed record of every statue on the island. They write descriptions, take photographs, map the locations, and collect other archaeological information. They use both old tools such as measuring tapes, compasses, and notebooks and newer technologies such as **GPS** (Global Positioning System) and other computer software. Archaeologists have learned a lot about Easter Island over the years, but some mysteries may never be completely solved.

SCIENCE SPOTLIGHT
A PECULIAR PATTERN

Hunt and Lipo used satellite imagery to map a system of ancient roads on Easter Island. Along these roads, they found abandoned statues. They noticed that many statues were lying facedown on roads sloping slightly downhill. Other statues were lying faceup on roads going slightly uphill. The abandoned statues seemed unfinished. Their bases were wide and angled, giving the statues a low center of gravity. Using physics and statistics, Hunt and Lipo calculated that the fallen statues must have started in a standing position. Statues being moved uphill would have naturally fallen on their backs. Those going downhill would have fallen on their faces. This research supported the theory that the statues were moved standing up rather than lying down.

An abandoned statue lies on its back near Ranu Raraku.

Timeline

400–1200	A small community of people from Polynesia settle on Easter Island.
700	The people of Easter Island begin carving giant statues from volcanic stone.
1600s	The islanders make the last of the Easter Island statues.
1722	Three Dutch ships commanded by Jacob Roggeveen visit and name Easter Island.
1888	Chile takes possession of Easter Island but leaves the statues alone.
1955–1956	Thor Heyerdahl conducts an experiment on Easter Island to determine whether the statues could have been moved on wooden sleds.
1995	The United Nations Educational, Scientific and Cultural Organization (UNESCO) names Easter Island a World Heritage Site.
2009	Jo Anne Van Tilburg begins excavating the buried statues on Easter Island and studying their markings.
2011	Terry Hunt and Carl Lipo show that Easter Island statues could have been moved using a simple rope system. This method makes a statue look as if it is walking.

GLOSSARY

archaeologists: people who study human history by digging up and studying ancient buildings, objects, and human remains

chisels: tools with a flat, sharp end to cut and shape a solid material such as stone

DNA: a substance that carries genetic information in the cells of plants and animals

eroded: destroyed by natural forces such as wind or water

excavate: to dig in the earth in search of buried remains

GPS: Global Positioning System, a system that uses satellite signals to determine an object's location or give directions to a location

monuments: a building or statue that honors a person or event

replica: an exact or very close copy of something

torsos: the main parts of human bodies, not including heads, arms, or legs

FURTHER INFORMATION

Easter Island
http://www.history.com/topics/easter-island

Niver, Heather Moore. *20 Fun Facts about Easter Island*. New York: Gareth Stevens, 2014.

O'Neal, Claire. *Polynesian Cultures in Perspective*. Hockessin, DE: Mitchell Lane, 2015.

Owings, Lisa. *Chile*. Minneapolis: Bellwether Media, 2012.

Polynesia
https://www.khanacademy.org/humanities/art-oceania/polynesia/a/polynesia-an-introduction

Polynesian Cultural Center: Rapa Nui (Easter Island)
http://www.polynesia.com/polynesian_culture/rapa-nui/#.WC4jwbIrKUk

"Scientists Make Easter Island Statue Walk"
https://www.youtube.com/watch?v=YpNuh-J5IgE

Weitzman, Elizabeth. *Mysteries of Stonehenge*. Minneapolis: Lerner Publications, 2018.

INDEX

PHOTO ACKNOWLEDGMENTS

The images in this book are used with the permission of: Gordan/Shutterstock.
com (design texture); © iStockphoto.com/Lindrik, p. 1; © Randy Olson/National
Geographic Magazines/Getty Images, pp. 4–5; © Anne Dirkse/Moment/Getty
Images, p. 6; © Look and Learn/Bridgeman Images, p. 7; © James L. Amos/Corbis
Documentary/Getty Images, pp. 8, 27; © Laura Westlund/Independent Picture
Service, p. 9; Douglas Peebles/Alamy Stock Photo, p. 10; © iStockphoto.com/
powerofforever, pp. 12, 25; © iStockphoto.com/TomazKunst, p. 13; © Steve_Allen/
Deposit Photos, p. 14; © VladimirKrupenkin/Deposit Photos, p. 15; © Weller/ullstein
bild/Getty Images, p. 16; Eric Lafforgue/Alamy Stock Photo, p. 17; © iStockphoto.com/
Mlenny, p. 18; © David LEFRANC/Gamma-Rapho/Getty Images, p. 19; © Bettmann/
Getty Images, p. 21; © Carl Lipo, pp. 22, 23; Gavin Hellier/Jon Arnold Images Ltd/
Alamy Stock Photo, p. 24; © Jan A. Martinsen/Aftenposten/NTB Scanpix/ZUMA
Press, p. 26; © De Agostini/W. Buss/Getty Images, p. 28.

Cover: © iStockphoto.com/Lindrik (main); Gordan/Shutterstock.com (texture).